A Primary Source Guide to

IRELAND

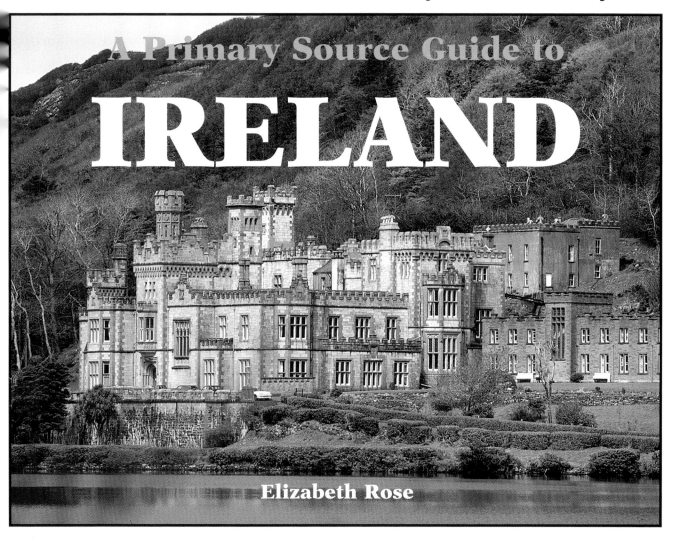

Elizabeth Rose

The Rosen Publishing Group's

PowerKids Press™
PRIMARY SOURCE

New York

For Emma Bean Destito, for whom the world has just begun

Published in 2004 by The Rosen Publishing Group, Inc.
29 East 21st Street, New York, NY 10010

First Edition

Editor: Natashya Wilson
Book Design: Haley Wilson
Book Layout: Maria E. Melendez
Photo Researcher: Adriana Skura

Photo Credits: Cover © Joe Viesti/The Viesti Collection, Inc; p. 4 © Geo Atlas; p. 5 © Cheryl Hogue/Britstock; p. 6 © Michael St. Maur Sheil/CORBIS; p. 7 © Graham Rice/GardenPhotos.com; p. 8 © Cheryl Hogue/Britstock; p. 8 (inset) © Ronald Gorbutt/Britstock; pp. 10, 16 © Hulton/Archive/Getty Images; pp. 10 (inset), 18 © Bettmann/CORBIS; p. 12 © AP/Wide World Photos; p. 14 © CORBIS; p. 17 High Cross at Kells, County Meath Ireland 9th century, photographed by William Lawrence (fl. 1870-80) (sepia photo) Private Collection/Bridgeman Art Library; p. 19 © Julian Calder/CORBIS; p. 20 © Tim Thompson/CORBIS p. 21 © Michael St. Maur Sheil/CORBIS.

Rose, Elizabeth.
A Primary Source Guide to Ireland / Elizabeth Rose.— 1st ed.
   v. cm.— (Countries of the World : A Primary Source Journey)
Includes bibliographical references and index.
Contents: The Emerald Isle—Soft weather—Early Irish history—Ireland and Northern Ireland—The Irish government—Ireland's economy—Religion in Ireland—The writers of Ireland—Irish traditions—Ireland at a glance.
ISBN 0-8239-6731-X (lib. bdg.)
1. Ireland—Juvenile literature. [1. Ireland.] I. Title. II. Series.
 DA906 .R665 2004
 941.7—dc21

                                                                          2002015648

Manufactured in the United States of America

Contents

SCOTLAND

UNITED

KINGDOM

Donegal

Northern
Ireland

•Belfast

•Sligo

*Irish
Sea*

Cashel

•Galway

•Kells

Dublin

IRELAND

ENGLAND

WALES

Cork •

NETHERLAN

BELGIUM

*Atlantic
Ocean*

FRANCE

4

The Emerald Isle

Ireland is a small island in the west of Europe, just off the coast of Great Britain. The island covers 32,052 square miles (83,014 sq km) of land. The

ancient Roman people called Ireland "Hibernia." Today Ireland has several nicknames. It is sometimes called by its Irish name, Éire, or by its nickname, Erin. Ireland is also known as the Emerald Isle because it is so green. The island of Ireland is split into two countries, Ireland and Northern Ireland. Northern Ireland is part of the United Kingdom. Ireland is its own country. It is also called the **Republic** of Ireland.

◀ The country of Ireland, not including Northern Ireland, covers 27,137 square miles (84,421 sq km) of land. *Above:* Ireland's greenery earned it the nickname the Emerald Isle. Ireland stays green year-round.

Soft Weather

Ireland usually has from 165 to 200 rainy days each year! Rainy days in Ireland are often misty, rather than stormy. The Irish people call this misty rain "soft weather." Ireland has an island **climate**. This means that warm, wet air from the Atlantic Ocean keeps the weather in Ireland mild and wet all year. Most of Ireland is rolling hills, pastures, and **wetlands**. The Burren is an area on the west coast that is made of giant plates of a rock called limestone. It covers 50 square miles (129 sq km) of land. This area has few trees, but many unusual plants and flowers grow in cracks in the rock.

◄ The Cliffs of Moher, shown on a soft weather day, rise 656 feet (200 m) above the sea and make up 5 miles (8 km) of Ireland's west coast.
Above: Bee orchids are some of the flowers that bloom in the Burren.

7

Early Irish History

The first people arrived on the island of Ireland 8,000 years ago. About 3,000 years ago, the **Celts** came from Europe. Most Irish people are **descendants** of the Celts. The **Vikings** ruled Ireland from 795 to 1014, when Celtic king Brian Boru won it from them. In 1169, **Norman** soldiers captured Ireland for England. From the 1530s to the 1800s, many English rulers tried to make the Irish people **Protestant** instead of **Catholic**. Laws were made to keep Catholics from owning land, voting, and practicing their religion. In 1801, Ireland and Great Britain became the United Kingdom. Catholics regained some rights, but many people were angry. They wanted their own country.

◀ Kings ruled from the Rock of Cashel from the 400s until 1101, when Cashel became part of the Catholic Church. *Inset:* The bones of about 25 people were found in Poulnabrone Dolmen, a tomb that dates from 2500 B.C.

the Irish signatories to a meeting summoned for the
purpose of the members elected to sit in the House of
Commons of Southern Ireland, and if approved shall be
ratified by the necessary legislation.

er 6ᵗʰ 1921

On behalf of the
British Delegation

D Lloyd George

Austen Chamberlain

Birkenhead.

Winston S. Churchill

L. Worthington-Evans

On behalf of the Irish
Delegation

Art ō Griobhtha (Arthur Griffith)

Mícheál Ó Coileáin

Riobárd Barton

E. S. Ó Dugáin

10

Ireland and Northern Ireland

On Easter Monday 1916, a group of Irish people began a war against the British government. It was called the Easter Rising. In 1921, Great Britain and Ireland signed the Anglo-Irish **Treaty**. This treaty made about 85 percent of Ireland the Irish Free State. This part was mostly Catholic people. The rest of the island became Northern Ireland. This part was mostly Protestant. Both were still part of the United Kingdom, but they had more freedom to govern themselves. From 1922 to 1923, Irish people who supported the treaty fought against those who did not. Thousands of people died. In 1937, the Irish Free State said that it was independent. In 1949, it officially became Ireland.

◀ Signers of the Anglo-Irish Treaty on December 6, 1921, included Irish patriot Michael Collins and British politician Winston Churchill. *Inset*: This picture from May 11, 1916, shows a building that was bombed during the Easter Rising.

The Irish Government

Ireland is run by a president, a **prime minister**, and a parliament. The president serves for seven years. He or she is elected by the people. The president's duties include calling Parliament to work and appointing a prime minister. The prime minister serves for up to five years. He or she manages how laws are put to use. Parliament, called the **Oireachtas**, has a house of representatives and a senate. The House of Representatives makes Ireland's laws. Its 166 members are elected by the Irish people. The Senate advises the prime minister and the House of Representatives. It has 60 members. They are chosen by others in Parliament, local Irish officials, and two of Ireland's universities.

◀ Mary Robinson (*right*) was the first woman president of Ireland. She served from 1990 to 1997, then became the United Nations High Commissioner for Human Rights. Here she is walking with her husband, Nick Robinson.

Ireland's Economy

In the 1800s, Ireland's economy depended on farming. Potatoes were the main crop. In 1845, all the potatoes went rotten from a disease. This caused a five-year **famine**. Millions of people died or left Ireland. The population dropped from about eight million to six million. The drop continued until the 1900s, when the newly growing economy helped people to stay. Today about four million people live in Ireland. Joining the **European Union** (E.U.) in 1973 helped Ireland to build its economy. Ireland's farm products include barley, cattle, and wheat. Manufacturing products include computers and clothing. Tourism is also growing. More than six million people visit the Emerald Isle each year.

◀ This drawing appeared in the *Illustrated London News* in 1851. It shows a priest offering blessings as an Irish family gets ready to leave Ireland.
Inset: Ireland began using the euro, the official money of the E.U., in 2002.

Religion in Ireland

Ninety-five percent of the people in Ireland are Roman Catholic. Five percent are Protestant or follow other beliefs. Most of the schools in Ireland are run by the Catholic Church, and most people go to church. Catholicism in Ireland dates from the fifth century A.D., when Saint Patrick brought the religion to the Celtic people.

An old story says that there are no snakes in Ireland because Patrick drove them all into the sea. Many churches claim to have been started by Saint Patrick. Today Saint Patrick is a patron saint of Ireland. Saint Patrick's Day is celebrated every year on March 17.

The Book of Kells was made by Catholic monks in Ireland around A.D. 806. This important religious artifact illustrates the four Gospels from the Bible. *Above:* Celtic crosses, such as this 9th-century cross, mark many Irish graves.

TRAVELS

INTO SEVERAL

Remote Nations

OF THE

WORLD.

In Four PARTS.

By *LEMUEL GULLIVER*,
First a Surgeon, and then a Captain of several SHIPS.

Vol. I.

LONDON·

Printed for Benj. Motte, *at the*
Middle Temple-Gate *in* Fleet-street.
MDCCXXVI.

Title-page of First Edition of "Gulliver's Travels"

18

The Writers of Ireland

Some of the world's greatest writers have come from Ireland. In 1726, Irishman Jonathan Swift's book *Gulliver's Travels* was published. It is one of the world's best-known children's books. Since 1923, four Irish writers have won the Nobel Prize for literature, the highest honor for a writer. These writers are poet William Butler Yeats, playwright George Bernard Shaw, playwright Samuel Beckett, and poet Seamus Heaney, from Northern Ireland. Irish writer James Joyce lived most of his life in Switzerland and Paris, but most of his stories take place in Ireland. He is one of Ireland's most famous writers.

This undated engraving shows Jonathan Swift. *Inset*: This is the title page from the first publishing of *Gulliver's Travels* in 1726. *Above*: Today novelists such as Edna O'Brien carry on Ireland's writing tradition.

Ireland Today

For centuries Ireland faced wars and troubled times, yet Ireland has held on to its **traditions**. The millions of Irish who moved away brought Irish culture to new places. Ireland has two official languages, modern English and ancient **Gaelic**, or  Irish. Shows such as *Riverdance* have made traditional Irish dance popular in many countries. The Irish still play traditional music and have also been successful in today's popular music. Irish bands such as Clannad and the rock band U2 are heard worldwide. Today about 30 percent of Ireland's population is younger than 25. The future of this growing country is bright.

◀ In Irish dance competitions, dancers wear costumes with beautiful Celtic designs, based on dress from 200 years ago. *Above:* Many places in Ireland have a band play nightly. Musicians play traditional instruments, including a drum called the bodhrán, shown in the upper left corner of this picture.

Population: 3,823,300

Capital City: Dublin, population 977,000

Largest City: Dublin

Official Names: Éire and Ireland

National Anthem: "The Soldier's Song"

Land Area: 27,137 square miles (84,421 sq km)

Government: Republic

Unit of Money: Euro

Flag: Three vertical bands of green, white, and orange. The green is for the Catholics, the orange is for the Protestants, and the white stands for the hope for peace between them.

Glossary

Catholic (KATH-lik) Someone who belongs to the Roman Catholic faith.

Celts (KELTS) Early European people who lived in the British Isles, Spain, and part of Asia.

climate (KLY-mit) The kind of weather a certain area has.

descendants (dih-SEN-dents) People born of a certain family or group.

European Union (yur-uh-PEE-in YOON-yun) A group of countries in Europe that work together to be friendly and to better their economies.

famine (FA-min) A shortage of food that causes people to starve.

Gaelic (GAY-lik) The Celtic languages of Ireland and Scotland. Irish Gaelic is usually called Irish.

Norman (NOR-mun) Of or about the people born or living in Normandy, France.

Oireachtas (er-OK-tus) Ireland's parliament, the group of elected leaders who make the laws.

prime minister (PRYM MIH-nih-ster) The leader of a government.

Protestant (PRAH-tes-tunt) A person who belongs to a Christian-based religion, but who is not Catholic.

republic (ree-PUB-lik) A government in which authority belongs to the people.

traditions (truh-DIH-shunz) Ways of doing things that have been passed down over time.

treaty (TREE-tee) An official agreement, signed by each party.

Vikings (VY-kingz) Scandinavian sailors who attacked the coasts of Europe from the eighth to the tenth centuries.

wetlands (WET-landz) Land with a lot of moisture in the soil.

Index

Primary Source List

Page 8. The Rock of Cashel, photographed by Cheryl Hogue in 1992. Kings ruled from the Rock from the 400s until 1101, when King Muircheartach O'Brien gave it to the Catholic Church. The oldest remaining part is the round tower, which dates from the twelfth centu

Page 8 (inset). Poulnabrone Dolmen, located in the Burren, photographed by Ronald Gorbutt in 1995. A major prehistoric site, this portal to dates from 2500 B.C. Bones of 1 infant, about 6 children, and 16–22 adults were recovered from the tomb.

Page 10. The signed Anglo-Irish Treaty, dated December 6, 1921. The British delegates included politician Winston Churchill, fourth signat on the left. The Irish delegates included patriot Michael Collins, second signature on the right, who was later assassinated.

Page 10 (inset). Ruins of a bombed building on Sackville Street in Dublin. Photographed on May 11, 1916, after the Easter Rising.

Page 14. Newspaper illustration from the *Illustrated London News*, 1851. A priest is blessing an Irish family before they leave Ireland.

Page 16. Pages from the Book of Kells, created by Irish monks, ca. A.D. 800. The book contains the four Gospels, written in Latin and illustrated with the world's finest existing example of Celtic art. The Book of Kells is kept at Trinity College in Dublin.

Page 17. Ninth-century Celtic high cross, located in County Meath. Photographed by William Lawrence, ca. 1870–80.

Page 18 (inset). Title page of the first edition of Jonathan Swift's *Gulliver's Travels*, 1726.

Page 20. Irish folk dancers in costume, photographed by Tim Thompson, 1991, in Skibbereen.

Page 21. Irish musicians at the Fleadh Cheoil Festival, an annual traditional music festival. Photographed August 16, 1995.

Web Sites

Due to the changing nature of Internet links, PowerKids Press has developed an online list of Web sites related to the subject of this book. This list is updated regularly. Please use this link to access the list:
www.powerkidslinks.com/cwpsj/irelan/